ESSENTIAL
Chinese

Contents

Introduction

Chinese cooking was for a long time unappreciated outside of China. Indeed, it was not until Chinese migrants settled in San Francisco during the Gold Rush period that Chinese food was introduced to the West. It was even longer before Chinese cuisine became noticed in Britain and Europe. Yet, since then its popularity has soared. Surprisingly however, Chinese cooking generally remains limited to specialist restaurants and trained professionals. It is only recently that some western cooks have tried it at home.

Yet Chinese cooking is the perfect choice for anyone wanting to cook at home. Not only is it healthy and nutritious but it is quick and easy to cook too. There are various methods of cooking Chinese-style. Steaming your food is the healthiest option as no fat is used in the cooking procedure. If you do not have a steamer, invert a heatproof plate in a large saucepan, add boiling water and cover with a lid or foil. Another option is stir-frying. Before you start cooking, cut your food into small pieces of similar size. Heat the wok before you add the oil. It will only take a few seconds for the oil to heat, add the ingredients and cook on full heat, stirring quickly and consistently until your meal is ready. You can also deep-fry in the wok. Less oil is required than with a standard deep-fryer and because of its shape, the oil actually drains from the food into the wok's centre.

If the health benefits of Chinese cooking are not enough to convert you, its history certainly will. For the majority of peasants in China life was extremely difficult. Food was extremely hard to find especially since natural disasters, such as floods and failed harvests were common. To appease hunger the Chinese often had to survive on rice or noodles alone. However, the Chinese cleverly created sauces such as, soy and hoi-sin, to add flavour to their food. Fuel supplies were also very low, so people learned to cook extremely quickly. To aid this cooking method they cut their food into very small pieces. Thus, stir-frying was invented.

However, Chinese cooking was not shaped by practicality alone. Philosophical and religious elements also played an important part in its development. The belief that everything in the universe is balanced and harmonious; where Yin balances Yang, day balances night and man balances woman is reflected in Chinese cooking. Therefore, the textures, colours and flavours of the ingredients should be balanced in order to create harmony.

Clear Chicken & Egg Soup

Serves 4

INGREDIENTS

1 tsp salt
1 tbsp rice wine vinegar
4 eggs
850 ml/1 1/2 pints/3 3/4 cups
  chicken stock

1 leek, sliced
125 g/4 1/2 oz broccoli florets
125 g/4 1/2 oz/1 cup shredded
  cooked chicken
2 open-cap mushrooms, sliced

1 tbsp dry sherry
dash of chilli sauce
chilli powder, to garnish

1 Bring a large saucepan of water to the boil and add the salt and rice wine vinegar. Reduce the heat so that it is just simmering and carefully break the eggs into the water, one at a time. Poach the eggs for 1 minute. Remove the poached eggs with a slotted spoon and set aside.

2 Bring the stock to the boil in a separate pan and add the leek, broccoli, chicken, mushrooms and sherry and season with chilli sauce to taste. Cook for 10–15 minutes.

3 Add the poached eggs to the soup and cook for a further 2 minutes. Carefully transfer the soup and poached eggs to 4 individual soup bowls. Dust with a little chilli powder to garnish and serve immediately.

COOK'S TIP

You could use 4 dried Chinese mushrooms, rehydrated according to the packet instructions, instead of the open-cap mushrooms, if you prefer.

VARIATION

You could substitute 125 g/4 1/2 oz fresh or canned crabmeat or the same quantity of fresh or frozen cooked prawns (shrimp) for the chicken, if desired.

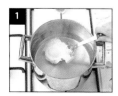

Beef & Vegetable Noodle Soup

Serves 4

INGREDIENTS

225 g/8 oz lean beef
1 garlic clove, crushed
2 spring onions (scallions), chopped
3 tbsp soy sauce

1 tsp sesame oil
225 g/8 oz egg noodles
850 ml/1¹/₂ pints/3³/₄ cups beef stock
3 baby corn cobs, sliced

¹/₂ leek, shredded
125 g/4¹/₂ oz broccoli, cut into florets (flowerets)
pinch of chilli powder

1 Using a sharp knife, cut the beef into thin strips and place them in a shallow glass bowl.

2 Add the garlic, spring onions (scallions), soy sauce and sesame oil and mix together well, turning the beef to coat. Cover and leave to marinate in the refrigerator for 30 minutes.

3 Cook the noodles in a saucepan of boiling water for 3–4 minutes. Drain the noodles thoroughly and set aside until required.

4 Put the beef stock in a large saucepan and bring to the boil.

5 Add the beef, together with the marinade, the baby corn, leek and broccoli. Cover and leave to simmer over a low heat for 7–10 minutes, or until the beef and vegetables are tender and cooked through.

6 Stir in the noodles and chilli powder and cook for a further 2–3 minutes. Transfer to bowls and serve immediately.

COOK'S TIP

Vary the vegetables used, or use those to hand. If preferred, use a few drops of chilli sauce instead of chilli powder, but remember it is very hot!

Curried Chicken & Sweetcorn (Corn) Soup

Serves 4

INGREDIENTS

175 g/6 oz can sweetcorn
(corn), drained
850 ml/1½ pints/3¾ cups
chicken stock
350 g/12 oz cooked, lean
chicken, cut into strips

16 baby corn cobs
1 tsp Chinese curry powder
1-cm/½-inch piece fresh root
ginger (ginger root), grated

3 tbsp light soy sauce
2 tbsp chopped chives

1 Place the canned sweetcorn (corn) in a food processor, together with 150 ml/¼ pint/⅔ cup of the chicken stock and process until the mixture forms a smooth purée.

2 Pass the sweetcorn purée through a fine sieve, pressing with the back of a spoon to remove any husks.

3 Pour the remaining chicken stock into a large pan and add the strips of cooked chicken. Stir in the sweetcorn (corn) purée.

4 Add the baby corn cobs and bring the soup to the boil. Boil the soup for 10 minutes.

5 Add the curry powder, ginger and soy sauce and cook for 10–15 minutes. Stir in the chives.

6 Transfer the soup to warm bowls and serve.

COOK'S TIP

Prepare the soup up to 24 hours in advance without adding the chicken, let cool, cover and store in the refrigerator. Add the chicken and heat the soup through thoroughly before serving.

Pancake Rolls

Serves 4

INGREDIENTS

4 tsp vegetable oil
1–2 garlic cloves, crushed
225 g/8 oz minced (ground) pork
225/8 oz pak choi, shredded

4½ tsp light soy sauce
½ tsp sesame oil
8 spring roll skins, 25 cm/ 10 inches square, thawed if frozen

oil, for deep-frying
chilli sauce (see Cook's Tip, below), to serve

1 Heat the vegetable oil in a preheated wok. Add the garlic and stir-fry for 30 seconds. Add the pork and stir-fry for 2–3 minutes, until just lightly coloured. Add the shredded pak choi, soy sauce and sesame oil to the wok and stir-fry for 2–3 minutes. Remove from the heat and set aside to cool.

2 Spread out the spring roll skins on a work surface (counter) and spoon 2 tbsp of the pork mixture along one edge of each. Roll the skin over

once and fold in the sides. Roll up completely to make a sausage shape, brushing the edges with a little water to seal. If you have time, set the pancake rolls aside for 10 minutes to seal firmly.

3 Heat the oil for deep-frying in a wok until almost smoking. Reduce the heat slightly and fry the pancake rolls, in batches if necessary, for 3–4 minutes, until golden. Remove from the oil with a slotted spoon and drain on kitchen paper (paper towels). Serve with chilli sauce.

COOK'S TIP

To make chilli sauce, heat 60 g/2 oz/¼ cup caster (superfine) sugar, 50 ml/2 fl oz/¼ cup rice vinegar and 2 tbsp water in a small pan, stirring until the sugar has dissolved. Bring the mixture to the boil and boil rapidly until a light syrup forms. Remove the pan from the heat and stir in 2 finely chopped, fresh red chillies. Leave the sauce to cool before serving. If you prefer a milder sauce, deseed the chillies before chopping them.

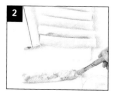

Sesame Prawn (Shrimp) Toasts

Serves 4

INGREDIENTS

225 g/8 oz cooked, peeled
    prawns (shrimp)
1 spring onion (scallion)
1/4 tsp salt
1 tsp light soy sauce

1 tbsp cornflour (cornstarch)
1 egg white, beaten
3 thin slices white bread,
    crusts removed
4 tbsp sesame seeds

vegetable oil, for deep-frying
chopped chives, to garnish

1 Put the prawns (shrimp) and spring onion (scallion) in a food processor and process until finely minced (ground). Alternatively, chop them very finely. Transfer to a bowl and stir in the salt, soy sauce, cornflour (cornstarch) and egg white.

2 Spread the mixture on to one side of each slice of bread. Spread the sesame seeds on top of the mixture, pressing down well.

3 Cut each slice into 4 equal triangles or strips.

4 Heat the oil for deep-frying in a wok until almost smoking. Carefully place the triangles in the oil, coated side down, and cook for 2–3 minutes, until golden brown. Remove with a slotted spoon and drain on kitchen paper (paper towels). Serve hot.

COOK'S TIP

Fry the triangles in two batches, keeping the first batch warm while you cook the second, to prevent them from overcooking.

VARIATION

If wished, you could add 1/2 tsp very finely chopped fresh root ginger and 1 tsp Chinese rice wine to the prawn (shrimp) mixture at the end of step 1.

Sweet & Sour Battered Prawns (Shrimp)

Serves 4

INGREDIENTS

16 large raw prawns (shrimp),
    peeled
1 tsp grated fresh root ginger
1 garlic clove, crushed
2 spring onions (scallions),
    sliced
2 tbsp dry sherry
2 tsp sesame oil
1 tbsp light soy sauce
vegetable oil, for deep-frying

shredded spring onion
    (scallion), to garnish

BATTER:
4 egg whites
4 tbsp cornflour (cornstarch)
2 tbsp plain (all-purpose) flour

SAUCE:
2 tbsp tomato purée
    (tomato paste)

3 tbsp white wine vinegar
4 tsp light soy sauce
2 tbsp lemon juice
3 tbsp light brown sugar
1 green (bell) pepper, seeded
    and cut into thin
    matchsticks
1/2 tsp chilli sauce
300 ml/1/2 pint/1 1/4 cups
    vegetable stock
2 tsp cornflour (cornstarch)

1 Using tweezers, devein the prawns (shrimp), then flatten them with a knife.

2 Place the prawns (shrimp) in a dish and add the ginger, garlic, spring onions (scallions), sherry, oil and soy. Cover and marinate for 30 minutes.

3 Make the batter by beating the egg whites until thick. Fold in the cornflour (cornstarch) and flour to form a light batter.

4 Place all of the sauce ingredients in a pan and bring to the boil. Reduce the heat and leave to simmer for 10 minutes.

5 Remove the prawns (shrimp) from the marinade and dip them into the batter to coat.

6 Heat the oil until almost smoking. Reduce the heat and fry the prawns (shrimp) for 3–4 minutes, until crisp. Serve with the sauce.

Spare Ribs

Serves 4

INGREDIENTS

900 g/2 lb pork spare ribs
2 tbsp dark soy sauce
3 tbsp hoisin sauce
1 tbsp Chinese rice wine or dry
   sherry

pinch of Chinese five spice
   powder
2 tsp dark brown sugar
1/4 tsp chilli sauce
2 garlic cloves, crushed

coriander (cilantro) sprigs, to
   garnish (optional)

1 Cut the spare ribs into separate pieces if they are joined together. If desired, you can chop them into 5 cm/2-inch lengths, using a cleaver.

2 Mix together the soy sauce, hoisin sauce, Chinese rice wine or sherry, Chinese five spice powder, dark brown sugar, chilli sauce and garlic.

3 Place the ribs in a shallow dish and pour the mixture over them, turning to coat them well. Cover and marinate in the

refrigerator, turning the ribs from time to time, for at least 1 hour.

4 Remove the ribs from the marinade and arrange them in a single layer on a wire rack placed over a roasting tin (pan) half filled with warm water. Brush with the marinade, reserving the remainder.

5 Cook in a preheated oven, at 180°C/350°F/ Gas Mark 4, for 30 minutes. Remove the roasting tin (pan) from the oven and turn the ribs over.

Brush with the remaining marinade and return to the oven for a further 30 minutes, or until cooked through. Transfer to a warmed serving dish, garnish with the coriander (cilantro) sprigs (if using) and serve immediately.

COOK'S TIP

Add more hot water to the roasting tin (pan) during cooking if required. Do not allow it to dry out as the water steams the ribs and aids in their cooking.

Steamed Fish with Black Bean Sauce

Serves 4

INGREDIENTS

900 g/2 lb whole snapper,
    cleaned and scaled
3 garlic cloves, crushed
2 tbsp black bean sauce
1 tsp cornflour (cornstarch)

2 tsp sesame oil
2 tbsp light soy sauce
2 tsp caster (superfine) sugar
2 tbsp dry sherry
1 small leek, shredded

1 small red (bell) pepper,
    seeded and cut into thin
    strips
shredded leek and lemon
    wedges, to garnish
boiled rice or noodles, to serve

1 Rinse the fish inside and out with cold running water and pat dry with kitchen paper (paper towels). Make 2–3 diagonal slashes in the flesh on each side of the fish, using a sharp knife. Rub the garlic into the fish.

2 Thoroughly mix the black bean sauce, cornflour (cornstarch), sesame oil, light soy sauce, sugar and dry sherry together in a bowl. Place the fish in a shallow heatproof dish and pour the sauce mixture over the top.

3 Sprinkle the leek and (bell) pepper strips on top of the sauce. Place the dish in the top of a steamer, cover and steam for 10 minutes, or until the fish is cooked through.

4 Transfer to a serving dish, garnish with shredded leek and lemon wedges and serve with boiled rice or noodles.

VARIATION

Whole sea bream or sea bass may be used in this recipe instead of snapper, if you prefer.

COOK'S TIP

Insert the point of a sharp knife into the fish to test if it is cooked. The fish is cooked through if the knife goes into the flesh easily.

Mullet with Ginger

Serves 4

INGREDIENTS

1 whole mullet, cleaned and scaled
2 spring onions (scallions), chopped
1 tsp grated fresh root ginger
125 ml/4 fl oz/$^1/_2$ cup garlic wine vinegar

125 ml/4 fl oz/$^1/_2$ cup light soy sauce
3 tsp caster (superfine) sugar
dash of chilli sauce
125 ml/4 fl oz/$^1/_2$ cup fish stock
1 green (bell) pepper, seeded and thinly sliced

1 large tomato, skinned, seeded and cut into thin strips
salt and pepper
sliced tomato, to garnish

1 Rinse the fish inside and out and pat dry with kitchen paper (paper towels).

2 Make 3 diagonal slits in the flesh on each side of the fish. Season with salt and pepper inside and out.

3 Place the fish on a heatproof plate and scatter the spring onions (scallions) and ginger over the top. Cover and steam for 10 minutes, or until the fish is cooked through.

4 Place the vinegar, soy sauce, sugar, chilli sauce, fish stock, (bell) pepper and tomato in a saucepan and bring to the boil, stirring occasionally. Cook over a high heat until the sauce has slightly reduced and thickened.

5 Remove the fish from the steamer and transfer to a warm serving dish. Pour the sauce over the fish, garnish with tomato slices and serve immediately.

COOK'S TIP

Use fillets of fish for this recipe if preferred, and reduce the cooking time to 5–7 minutes.

Szechuan White Fish

Serves 4

INGREDIENTS

350 g/12 oz white fish fillets
1 small egg, beaten
3 tbsp plain (all-purpose) flour
4 tbsp dry white wine
3 tbsp light soy sauce
vegetable oil, for frying
1 garlic clove, cut into slivers
1-cm/^{1}/2-inch piece fresh root
    ginger, finely chopped

1 onion, finely chopped
1 celery stick, chopped
1 fresh red chilli, chopped
3 spring onions (scallions),
    chopped
1 tsp rice wine vinegar
^{1}/2 tsp ground Szechuan
    pepper

175 ml/6 fl oz/^{3}/4 cup fish
    stock
1 tsp caster (superfine) sugar
1 tsp cornflour (cornstarch)
2 tsp water
chilli flowers and celery leaves,
    to garnish (optional)

1 Cut the fish into 4-cm/
1½-inch cubes.

2 In a bowl, beat the egg,
flour, wine and 1 tbsp of
soy sauce to make a batter.

3 Dip the cubes of fish
into the batter to coat.

4 Heat the oil in a
preheated wok until it
is almost smoking. Reduce
the heat slightly and cook
the fish, in batches, for
2–3 minutes, until golden.
Drain on kitchen paper
(paper towels) and set aside.

5 Pour all but 1 tbsp of
oil from the wok and
return to the heat. Add the
garlic, ginger, onion, celery,
chilli and spring onions
(scallions) and stir-fry for
1–2 minutes.

6 Stir in the remaining
soy sauce and the
vinegar.

7 Add the Szechuan
pepper, fish stock and
sugar to the wok. Blend
the cornflour (cornstarch)
with the water to form a
smooth paste and stir it
into the stock. Bring to the
boil and cook, stirring, for
1 minute, until the sauce
thickens and clears.

8 Return the fish to the
wok and cook for
1–2 minutes, until hot.
Transfer to a serving dish.

Cantonese Prawns (Shrimp)

Serves 4

INGREDIENTS

5 tbsp vegetable oil
4 garlic cloves, crushed
675 g/1 1/2 lb raw prawns
  (shrimp), shelled and
  deveined
5-cm/2-inch piece fresh root
  ginger, chopped
175 g/6 oz lean pork, diced

1 leek, sliced
3 eggs, beaten
shredded leek and red (bell)
  pepper matchsticks, to
  garnish

SAUCE:
2 tbsp dry sherry
2 tbsp light soy sauce
2 tsp caster (superfine) sugar
150 ml/1/4 pint/2/3 cup fish
  stock
4 1/2 tsp cornflour (cornstarch)
3 tbsp water

1 Heat 2 tablespoons of the oil in a preheated wok. Add the garlic and stir-fry for 30 seconds. Add the prawns (shrimp) and stir-fry for 5 minutes, or until they change colour. Remove the prawns (shrimp) from the wok with a slotted spoon, set aside and keep warm.

2 Add the remaining oil to the wok and heat. Add the ginger, diced pork and leek and stir-fry over a medium heat for 4–5 minutes, or until the pork is lightly coloured.

3 Add the sherry, soy, sugar and fish stock to the wok. Blend the cornflour (cornstarch) with the water to form a smooth paste and stir it into the wok. Cook, stirring, until the sauce thickens and clears.

4 Return the prawns (shrimp) to the wok and add the beaten eggs.

Cook for 5–6 minutes, gently stirring occasionally, until the eggs set. Transfer to a warm serving dish, garnish with shredded leek and (bell) pepper matchsticks and serve immediately.

COOK'S TIP

If possible, use Chinese rice wine instead of the sherry.

Chilli Chicken

Serves 4

INGREDIENTS

350 g/12 oz skinless, boneless
lean chicken
$^1/_2$ tsp salt
1 egg white, lightly beaten
2 tbsp cornflour (cornstarch)
4 tbsp vegetable oil
2 garlic cloves, crushed

1-cm/$^1/_2$-inch piece fresh root
ginger, grated
1 red (bell) pepper, seeded and
diced
1 green (bell) pepper, seeded
and diced
2 fresh red chillies, chopped

2 tbsp light soy sauce
1 tbsp dry sherry or Chinese
rice wine
1 tbsp wine vinegar

1 Cut the chicken into cubes and place in a mixing bowl. Add the salt, egg white, cornflour (cornstarch) and 1 tbsp of the oil. Turn the chicken in the mixture to coat well.

2 Heat the remaining oil in a preheated wok. Add the garlic and ginger and stir-fry for 30 seconds.

3 Add the chicken pieces to the wok and stir-fry for 2–3 minutes, or until browned.

4 Stir in the (bell) peppers, chillies, soy sauce, sherry or Chinese rice wine and wine vinegar and cook for 2–3 minutes, until the chicken is cooked through. Transfer to a serving dish and serve.

VARIATION

This recipe works well if you use 350 g/12 oz lean steak, cut into thin strips or 450 g/ 1 lb raw prawns (shrimp) instead of the chicken.

COOK'S TIP

When preparing chillies, wear rubber gloves to prevent the juices from burning and irritating your hands. Be careful not to touch your face, especially your lips or eyes, until you have washed your hands.

Lemon Chicken

Serves 4

INGREDIENTS

vegetable oil, for deep-frying
650 g/1¹/₂ lb skinless, boneless
    chicken, cut into strips
lemon slices and shredded
    spring onions (scallions),
    to garnish

SAUCE:
1 tbsp cornflour (cornstarch)
6 tbsp cold water
3 tbsp fresh lemon juice
2 tbsp sweet sherry
¹/₂ tsp caster (superfine) sugar

1 Heat the oil in a wok until almost smoking. Reduce the heat and stir-fry the chicken strips for 3–4 minutes, until cooked through. Remove the chicken with a slotted spoon, set aside and keep warm. Drain the oil from the wok.

2 To make the sauce, mix the cornflour with 2 tablespoons of the water to form a paste.

3 Pour the lemon juice and remaining water into the mixture in the wok. Add the sherry and sugar and bring to the boil, stirring until the sugar has completely dissolved.

4 Stir in the cornflour mixture and return to the boil. Reduce the heat and simmer, stirring constantly, for 2–3 minutes, until the sauce is thickened and clear.

5 Transfer the chicken to a warm serving plate and pour the sauce over the top. Garnish with the lemon slices and shredded spring onions (scallions) and serve immediately.

COOK'S TIP

If you would prefer to use chicken portions rather than strips, cook them in the oil, covered, over a low heat for about 30 minutes, or until cooked through.

Chicken With Cashew Nuts & Vegetables

Serves 4

INGREDIENTS

300 g/10 1/2 oz boneless,
  skinless chicken breasts
1 tbsp cornflour (cornstarch)
1 tsp sesame oil
1 tbsp hoisin sauce
1 tsp light soy sauce
3 garlic cloves, crushed
2 tbsp vegetable oil

75 g/2 3/4 oz/3/4 cup unsalted
  cashew nuts
25 g/1 oz mangetout (snow
  peas)
1 celery stick, sliced
1 onion, cut into 8 pieces
60 g/2 oz beansprouts

1 red (bell) pepper, seeded and
  diced

SAUCE:
2 tsp cornflour (cornstarch)
2 tbsp hoisin sauce
200 ml/7 fl oz/7/8 cup chicken
  stock

1 Trim any fat from the chicken breasts and cut the meat into thin strips. Place the chicken in a large bowl. Sprinkle with the cornflour (cornstarch) and toss to coat the chicken strips in it, shaking off any excess. Mix together the sesame oil, hoisin sauce, soy sauce and 1 garlic clove. Pour this mixture over the chicken, turning to coat. Marinate for 20 minutes.

2 Heat half of the vegetable oil in a preheated wok. Add the cashew nuts and stir-fry for 1 minute, until browned. Add the mangetout (snow peas), celery, the remaining garlic, the onion, bean-sprouts and red (bell) pepper and cook, stirring occasionally, for 2–3 minutes. Remove the vegetables from the wok with a slotted spoon, set aside and keep warm.

3 Heat the remaining oil in the wok. Remove the chicken from the marinade and stir-fry for 3–4 minutes. Return the vegetables to the wok.

4 To make the sauce, mix the cornflour (cornstarch), hoisin sauce and chicken stock and pour into the wok. Bring to the boil, stirring until thickened and clear. Serve.

Chicken with Yellow Bean Sauce

Serves 4

INGREDIENTS

450 g/1 lb skinless, boneless
   chicken breasts
1 egg white, beaten
1 tbsp cornflour (cornstarch)
1 tbsp rice wine vinegar
1 tbsp light soy sauce

1 tsp caster (superfine) sugar
3 tbsp vegetable oil
1 garlic clove, crushed
1-cm/$\frac{1}{2}$-inch piece fresh root
   ginger, grated

1 green (bell) pepper, seeded
   and diced
2 large mushrooms, sliced
3 tbsp yellow bean sauce
yellow or green (bell) pepper
   strips, to garnish

1 Trim any fat from the chicken. Cut the meat into 2.5-cm/1-inch cubes.

2 Mix the egg white and cornflour (cornstarch) in a shallow bowl. Add the chicken and turn in the mixture to coat. Set aside for 20 minutes.

3 Mix the vinegar, soy sauce and sugar in a bowl.

4 Remove the chicken from the egg white mixture.

5 Heat the oil in a preheated wok, add the chicken and stir-fry for 3–4 minutes, until golden brown. Remove the chicken from the wok with a slotted spoon, set aside and keep warm.

6 Add the garlic, ginger, (bell) pepper and mushrooms to the wok and stir-fry for 1–2 minutes.

7 Add the yellow bean sauce and cook for 1 minute. Stir in the vinegar mixture and return the chicken to the wok. Cook for 1–2 minutes and serve hot, garnished with (bell) pepper strips.

VARIATION

Black bean sauce would work equally well with this recipe. Although this would affect the appearance of the dish, as it is much darker in colour, the flavours would be compatible.

Spicy Peanut Chicken

Serves 4

INGREDIENTS

300 g/10^1/$_2$ oz skinless,
   boneless chicken breast
2 tbsp peanut oil
125 g/4^1/$_2$ oz/1 cup shelled
   peanuts
1 fresh red chilli, sliced
1 green (bell) pepper, seeded
   and cut into strips

1 tsp sesame oil
fried rice, to serve

SAUCE:
150 ml/^{1}/$_4$ pint/^{2}/$_3$ cup
   chicken stock
1 tbsp Chinese rice wine or
   dry sherry

1 tbsp light soy sauce
1^1/$_2$ tsp light brown sugar
2 garlic cloves, crushed
1 tsp grated fresh root ginger
1 tsp rice wine vinegar

---

1 Trim any fat from the chicken and cut the meat into 2.5-cm/ 1-inch cubes. Set aside.

2 Heat the peanut oil in a preheated wok. Add the peanuts and stir-fry for 1 minute. Remove the peanuts with a slotted spoon and set aside.

3 Add the chicken to the wok and cook for 1–2 minutes. Stir in the chilli and (bell) pepper and cook

for 1 minute. Remove from the wok with a slotted spoon.

4 Put half of the peanuts in a food processor and process until almost smooth. Alternatively, place them in a plastic bag and crush with a rolling pin.

5 To make the sauce, add the chicken stock, Chinese rice wine or dry sherry, soy sauce, sugar, garlic, ginger and rice wine vinegar to the wok.

6 Heat the sauce without boiling and stir in the peanut purée, remaining peanuts, chicken, chilli and (bell) pepper. Sprinkle with the sesame oil, stir and cook for 1 minute. Serve hot.

COOK'S TIP

If necessary, process the peanuts with a little of the stock in step 4 to form a softer paste.

Peking Duck

Serves 4

INGREDIENTS

1.8 kg/4 lb duck	2 tbsp sesame oil	125 ml/4 fl oz/^{1}/2 cup water
1.75 litres/3 pints/7^1/2 cups boiling water	125 ml/4 fl oz/^{1}/2 cup hoisin sauce	carrot strips, to garnish
4 tbsp clear honey	125 g/4^1/2 oz/^{2}/3 cup caster (superfine) sugar	Chinese pancakes, cucumber matchsticks and spring onions (scallions), to serve
2 tsp dark soy sauce		

1 Place the duck on a rack set over a roasting tin (pan) and pour 1.2 litres/ 2 pints/5 cups of the boiling water over it. Remove the duck and rack and discard the water. Pat dry with paper towels, replace the duck and the rack and set aside for several hours.

2 Mix together the honey, remaining boiling water and soy sauce. Brush the mixture over the skin and inside the duck. Reserve the remaining glaze. Set the

duck aside for 1 hour, until the glaze has dried.

3 Coat the duck with another layer of glaze. Let dry and repeat until all of the glaze is used.

4 Heat the oil and add the hoisin sauce, sugar and water. Simmer for 2–3 minutes, until thickened. Cool and refrigerate.

5 Cook the duck in a preheated oven, at 190°C/375°F/Gas Mark 5, for 30 minutes. Turn the duck over and cook for

20 minutes. Turn the duck again and cook for 20–30 minutes, or until cooked through and the skin is crisp.

6 Remove the duck from the oven and set aside for 10 minutes. Meanwhile, heat the pancakes in a steamer for 5–7 minutes. Cut the skin and duck meat into strips, garnish with the carrot strips and serve with the pancakes, sauce, cucumber and spring onions (scallions).

Honey-glazed Duck

Serves 4

INGREDIENTS

1 tsp dark soy sauce
2 tbsp clear honey
1 tsp garlic vinegar
2 garlic cloves, crushed
1 tsp ground star anise

2 tsp cornflour (cornstarch)
2 tsp water
2 large boneless duck breasts, about 225g/8 oz each

TO GARNISH:
celery leaves
cucumber wedges
snipped chives

1 Mix the soy sauce, clear honey, garlic vinegar, garlic and star anise. Blend the cornflour (cornstarch) with the water to form a smooth paste and stir it into the mixture.

2 Place the duck breasts in a shallow ovenproof dish. Brush with the soy marinade, turning to coat them completely. Cover and leave to marinate in the refrigerator for at least 2 hours, or overnight.

3 Remove the duck from the marinade and cook in a preheated oven, at 220°C/425°F/Gas Mark 7, for 20–25 minutes, basting frequently with the glaze.

4 Remove the duck from the oven and transfer to a preheated grill (broiler). Grill (broil) for about 3–4 minutes to caramelize the top.

5 Remove the duck from the grill (broiler) pan and cut into thin slices. Arrange the duck slices in a warm serving dish, garnish with celery leaves, cucumber wedges and snipped chives and serve immediately.

COOK'S TIP

If the duck begins to burn slightly while it is cooking in the oven, cover with foil. Check that the duck breasts are cooked through by inserting the point of a sharp knife into the thickest part of the flesh – the juices should run clear.

Stir-Fried Duck with Broccoli & (Bell) Peppers

Serves 4

INGREDIENTS

1 egg white
2 tbsp cornflour (cornstarch)
450 g/1 lb skinless, boneless
  duck meat
vegetable oil, for deep-frying
1 red (bell) pepper, seeded and
  diced

1 yellow (bell) pepper, seeded
  and diced
125 g/4^1/2 oz small broccoli
  florets
1 garlic clove, crushed
2 tbsp light soy sauce

2 tsp Chinese rice wine or dry
  sherry
1 tsp light brown sugar
125 ml/4 fl oz/^{1}/2 cup chicken
  stock
2 tsp sesame seeds

1 Beat the egg white and cornflour (cornstarch) together in a mixing bowl.

2 Cut the duck meat into cubes and stir into the egg white mixture. Let stand for 30 minutes.

3 Heat the oil for deep-frying in a wok until almost smoking. Remove the duck from the egg white mixture, add to the wok and fry in the oil for

4–5 minutes, until crisp. Remove the duck from the oil and drain on kitchen paper (paper towels).

4 Add the (bell) peppers and broccoli to the wok and fry for 2–3 minutes. Remove with a slotted spoon and drain on kitchen paper (paper towels).

5 Pour all but 2 tbsp of the oil from the wok and return to the heat. Add

the garlic and stir-fry for 30 seconds. Stir in the soy sauce, Chinese rice wine or sherry, sugar and stock and bring to the boil.

6 Stir in the duck and reserved vegetables and cook for 1–2 minutes.

7 Carefully spoon the duck and vegetables on to a warmed serving dish and sprinkle with the sesame seeds. Serve.

Pork Fry with Vegetables

Serves 4

INGREDIENTS

350 g/12 oz lean pork
fillet (tenderloin)
2 tbsp vegetable oil
2 garlic cloves, crushed
1-cm/^{1}/2-inch piece fresh root
ginger, cut into slivers
1 carrot, cut into thin strips

1 red (bell) pepper, seeded and
diced
1 fennel bulb, sliced
25 g/1 oz water chestnuts,
halved
75 g/2 ^{3}/4 oz beansprouts
2 tbsp Chinese rice wine

300 ml/^{1}/2 pint/1^{1}/4 cups pork
or chicken stock
pinch of dark brown sugar
1 tsp cornflour (cornstarch)
2 tsp water

1 Cut the pork into thin slices. Heat the oil in a preheated wok. Add the garlic, ginger and pork and stir-fry for 1–2 minutes, until the meat is sealed.

2 Add the carrot, (bell) pepper, fennel and water chestnuts to the wok and stir-fry for 2–3 minutes.

3 Add the beansprouts and stir-fry for 1 minute. Remove the pork and vegetables from the wok and keep warm.

4 Add the Chinese rice wine, pork or chicken stock and sugar to the wok. Blend the cornflour (cornstarch) to a smooth paste with the water and stir it into the sauce. Bring to the boil, stirring, until thickened and clear.

5 Return the meat and vegetables to the wok and cook for 1–2 minutes, until heated through and coated with the sauce. Transfer to a warm serving dish and serve immediately.

COOK'S TIP

Use dry sherry instead of the Chinese rice wine if you have difficulty obtaining it.

Sweet & Sour Pork

Serves 4

INGREDIENTS

150 ml/^{1}/$_4$ pint/^{2}/$_3$ cup
   vegetable oil, for deep-
   frying
225 g/8 oz pork fillet
   (tenderloin), cut into
   1-cm/^{1}/$_2$-inch cubes
1 onion, sliced
1 green (bell) pepper, seeded
   and sliced
225 g/8 oz pineapple pieces
1 small carrot, cut into thin
   strips

25 g/1 oz canned bamboo
   shoots, drained, rinsed and
   halved
rice or noodles, to serve

BATTER:
125 g/4^1/$_2$ oz/1 cup plain (all-
   purpose) flour
1 tbsp cornflour (cornstarch)
1^1/$_2$ tsp baking powder
1 tbsp vegetable oil

SAUCE:
125 g/4^1/$_2$ oz/ ^{2}/$_3$ cup light
   brown sugar
2 tbsp cornflour (cornstarch)
125 ml/4 fl oz/^{1}/$_2$ cup white
   wine vinegar
2 garlic cloves, crushed
4 tbsp tomato purée (paste)
6 tbsp pineapple juice

1 To make the batter, sift the flour into a bowl, together with the cornflour (cornstarch) and baking powder. Add the oil and stir in enough water to make a thick batter (about 175 ml/ 6 fl oz/ ^{3}/$_4$ cup). Pour the vegetable oil into a wok and heat until almost smoking. Dip the cubes of pork into the batter, and cook in the hot oil, in batches, until the pork is cooked through. Remove the pork from the wok, set aside and keep warm. Drain all but 1 tbsp of oil from the wok and return it to the heat. Add the onion, (bell) pepper, pineapple pieces, carrot and bamboo shoots and stir-fry for 1–2 minutes. Remove from the wok and set aside.

2 Mix all of the sauce ingredients together and pour into the wok. Bring to the boil, stirring until thickened and clear. Cook for 1 minute, then return the pork and vegetables to the wok. Cook for 1–2 minutes, then transfer to a serving plate and serve.

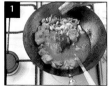

Pork with Plums

Serves 4

INGREDIENTS

450 g/1 lb pork fillet
(tenderloin)
1 tbsp cornflour (cornstarch)
2 tbsp light soy sauce
2 tbsp Chinese rice wine
4 tsp light brown sugar

pinch of ground cinnamon
5 tsp vegetable oil
2 garlic cloves, crushed
2 spring onions (scallions),
chopped
4 tbsp plum sauce

1 tbsp hoisin sauce
150 ml/¼ pint/⅔ cup water
dash of chilli sauce
fried plum quarters and spring
onions (scallions), to
garnish

1 Cut the pork fillet (tenderloin) into slices.

2 Mix the cornflour (cornstarch), soy sauce, rice wine, sugar and cinnamon together.

3 Place the pork in a shallow dish and pour the cornflour (cornstarch) mixture over it. Cover and leave to marinate for at least 30 minutes.

4 Remove the pork from the dish, reserving the marinade.

5 Heat the oil in a preheated wok. Add the pork and stir-fry for 3–4 minutes, until lightly coloured.

6 Stir in the garlic, spring onions (scallions), plum sauce, hoisin sauce, water and chilli sauce. Bring the sauce to the boil. Reduce the heat, cover and simmer for 8–10 minutes, or until the pork is cooked through and tender.

7 Stir in the reserved marinade and cook,

stirring, for 5 minutes. Transfer to a warm serving dish and garnish with fried plum quarters and spring onions (scallions). Serve immediately.

VARIATION

Strips of boneless duck meat may be used instead of the pork, if you prefer.

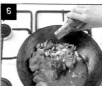

Marinated Beef With Oyster Sauce

Serves 4

INGREDIENTS

225 g/8 oz lean steak, cut into
    2.5-cm/1-inch cubes
1 tbsp light soy sauce
1 tsp sesame oil
2 tsp Chinese rice wine or
    dry sherry
1 tsp caster (superfine)
    sugar
2 tsp hoisin sauce
1 garlic clove, crushed
$^1/_2$ tsp cornflour (cornstarch)

green (bell) pepper slices,
    to garnish
rice or noodles, to serve

SAUCE:
2 tbsp dark soy sauce
1 tsp caster (superfine) sugar
$^1/_2$ tsp cornflour (cornstarch)
3 tbsp oyster sauce
8 tbsp water
2 tbsp vegetable oil

3 garlic cloves, crushed
1-cm/$^1/_2$-inch piece fresh root
    ginger, grated
8 baby corn cobs, halved
    lengthways
$^1/_2$ green (bell) pepper, seeded
    and thinly sliced
25 g/1 oz bamboo shoots,
    drained and rinsed

1 Place the steak in a shallow dish. Mix together the soy sauce, sesame oil, Chinese rice wine or sherry, sugar, hoisin sauce, garlic and cornflour (cornstarch) and pour over the steak, turning it to coat. Cover and marinate for at least 1 hour.

2 To make the sauce, mix the dark soy sauce with the sugar, cornflour (cornstarch), oyster sauce and water. Heat the oil in a wok. Add the steak and the marinade and stir-fry for 2–3 minutes, until sealed and lightly browned.

3 Add the garlic, ginger, baby corn cobs, (bell) pepper and bamboo shoots. Stir in the oyster sauce mixture and bring to the boil. Reduce the heat and cook for 2–3 minutes. Transfer to a warm serving dish, garnish with green (bell) pepper slices and serve immediately.

COOK'S TIP

For a fuller flavour, marinate the beef in the refrigerator overnight.

Spicy Beef

Serves 4

INGREDIENTS

225 g/8 oz fillet steak
2 garlic cloves, crushed
1 tsp powdered star anise
1 tbsp dark soy sauce
spring onion (scallion) tassels,
   to garnish

SAUCE:
2 tbsp vegetable oil
1 bunch spring onions
   (scallions), halved
   lengthways
1 tbsp dark soy sauce

1 tbsp dry sherry
$^1/_4$ tsp chilli sauce
150 ml/$^1/_4$ pint/$^2/_3$ cup water
2 tsp cornflour (cornstarch)
4 tsp water

1 Cut the steak into thin strips and place in a shallow dish.

2 Mix together the garlic, star anise and dark soy sauce in a bowl and pour over the steak strips, turning them to coat thoroughly. Cover and leave to marinate in the refrigerator for at least 1 hour.

3 To make the sauce, heat the oil in a preheated wok. Reduce the heat, add the halved spring onions (scallions) and stir-fry for 1–2 minutes. Remove from the wok with a slotted spoon and set aside.

4 Add the beef to the wok, together with the marinade, and stir-fry for 3–4 minutes. Return the halved spring onions (scallions) to the wok and add the soy sauce, sherry, chilli sauce and two thirds of the water.

5 Blend the cornflour (cornstarch) with the remaining water and stir into the wok. Bring to the boil, stirring until the sauce thickens and clears.

6 Transfer to a warm serving dish, garnish with spring onion (scallion) tassels and serve immediately.

COOK'S TIP

Omit the chilli sauce for a milder dish.

Lamb with Mushroom Sauce

Serves 4

INGREDIENTS

350 g/12 oz lean boneless
  lamb, such as fillet or loin
2 tbsp vegetable oil
3 garlic cloves, crushed
1 leek, sliced

1 tsp cornflour (cornstarch)
4 tbsp light soy sauce
3 tbsp Chinese rice wine or
  dry sherry
3 tbsp water

$^{1}/_{2}$ tsp chilli sauce
175 g/6 oz large mushrooms,
  sliced
$^{1}/_{2}$ tsp sesame oil
fresh red chillies, to garnish

1 Cut the lamb into thin strips.

2 Heat the oil in a preheated wok. Add the lamb strips, garlic and leek and stir-fry for about 2–3 minutes.

3 Mix together the cornflour (cornstarch), soy sauce, Chinese rice wine or dry sherry, water and chilli sauce in a bowl and set aside.

4 Add the mushrooms to the wok and stir-fry for 1 minute.

5 Stir in the sauce and cook for 2–3 minutes, or until the lamb is cooked through and tender. Sprinkle the sesame oil over the top and transfer to a warm serving dish. Garnish with red chillies and serve immediately.

COOK'S TIP

Use rehydrated dried Chinese mushrooms obtainable from specialist shops or Chinese supermarkets for a really authentic flavour.

VARIATION

The lamb can be replaced with lean steak or pork fillet (tenderloin) in this classic recipe from Beijing. You could also use 2–3 spring onions (scallions), 1 shallot or 1 small onion instead of the leek, if you prefer.

Lamb with Garlic Sauce

Serves 4

INGREDIENTS

450 g/1 lb lamb fillet or loin
2 tbsp dark soy sauce
2 tsp sesame oil
2 tbsp Chinese rice wine or dry
  sherry

$^{1}/_{2}$ tsp Szechuan pepper
4 tbsp vegetable oil
4 garlic cloves, crushed
60 g/2 oz water chestnuts,
  quartered

1 green (bell) pepper, seeded
  and sliced
1 tbsp wine vinegar
1 tbsp sesame oil
rice or noodles, to serve

1 Cut the lamb into 2.5-cm/1-inch pieces and place in a shallow dish.

2 Mix together 1 tbsp of the soy sauce, the sesame oil, Chinese rice wine or sherry and Szechuan pepper. Pour the mixture over the lamb, turning to coat, and leave to marinate for 30 minutes.

3 Heat the vegetable oil in a preheated wok. Remove the lamb from the marinade and add to the wok with the garlic. Stir-fry for 2–3 minutes.

4 Add the water chestnuts and (bell) pepper to the wok and stir-fry for 1 minute.

5 Add the remaining soy sauce and the wine vinegar, mixing well.

6 Add the sesame oil and cook, stirring, for 1–2 minutes, or until the lamb is cooked through.

7 Transfer the lamb and garlic sauce to a warm serving dish and serve immediately with rice or noodles.

COOK'S TIP

Sesame oil is used as a flavouring, rather than for frying, as it burns readily, hence it is added at the end of cooking.

VARIATION

Chinese chives, also known as garlic chives, would make an appropriate garnish for this dish.

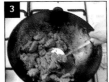
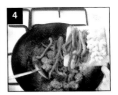

Hot Lamb

Serves 4

INGREDIENTS

450 g/1 lb lean, boneless lamb

2 tbsp hoisin sauce

1 tbsp dark soy sauce

1 garlic clove, crushed

2 tsp grated fresh root ginger

2 tbsp vegetable oil

2 onions, sliced

1 fennel bulb, sliced

4 tbsp water

SAUCE:

1 large fresh red chilli, cut into
   thin strips

1 fresh green chilli, cut into
   thin strips

2 tbsp rice wine vinegar

2 tsp light brown sugar

2 tbsp peanut oil

1 tsp sesame oil

1 Cut the lamb into 2.5-cm/1-inch cubes and place in a shallow glass dish.

2 Mix together the hoisin sauce, soy sauce, garlic and ginger in a bowl and pour over the lamb, turning to coat well. Leave to marinate in the refrigerator for 20 minutes.

3 Heat the vegetable oil in a preheated wok. Add the lamb and stir-fry for 1–2 minutes.

4 Add the onions and fennel to the wok and cook for a further 2 minutes, or until they are just beginning to brown.

5 Stir in the water, cover and cook for 2–3 minutes.

6 To make the sauce, place the chillies, rice wine vinegar, sugar, peanut oil and sesame oil in a saucepan and cook over a low heat for 3-4 minutes, stirring to combine.

7 Transfer the lamb and onions to a warm serving dish, pour the sauce on top, toss lightly and serve immediately.

VARIATION

Use beef, pork or duck instead of the lamb and vary the vegetables, using leeks or celery instead of the onion and fennel.

Sesame Lamb Stir-Fry

Serves 4

INGREDIENTS

450 g/1 lb boneless lean lamb
2 tbsp peanut oil
2 leeks, sliced
1 carrot, cut into matchsticks

2 garlic cloves, crushed
3 fl oz/85 ml/^{1}/3 cup lamb or
   vegetable stock
2 tsp light brown sugar

1 tbsp dark soy sauce
4^1/2 tsp sesame seeds

1 Cut the lamb into thin strips. Heat the peanut oil in a preheated wok. Add the lamb and stir-fry for 2–3 minutes. Remove the lamb from the wok with a slotted spoon and set aside.

2 Add the leek, carrot and garlic to the wok and stir-fry in the remaining oil for 1–2 minutes. Remove from the wok with a slotted spoon and set aside. Drain any oil from the wok.

3 Place the stock, sugar and soy sauce in the wok and add the lamb.

Cook, stirring constantly to coat the lamb, for 2–3 minutes. Sprinkle the sesame seeds over the top, turning the lamb to coat.

4 Spoon the leek mixture on to a warm serving dish and top with the lamb. Serve immediately.

COOK'S TIP

Be careful not to burn the sugar in the wok when heating and coating the meat, otherwise the flavour of the dish will be spoiled.

VARIATION

This recipe would be equally delicious made with strips of skinless chicken or turkey breast or with prawns (shrimp). The cooking times remain the same.

Egg Fried Rice

Serves 4

INGREDIENTS

150 g/5^1/2 oz/^{2}/3 cup long-
  grain rice
3 eggs, beaten
2 tbsp vegetable oil
2 garlic cloves, crushed

4 spring onions (scallions),
  chopped
125 g/4^1/2 oz/1 cup cooked
  peas
1 tbsp light soy sauce

pinch of salt
shredded spring onion
  (scallion), to garnish

1 Cook the rice in a saucepan of boiling water for 10–12 minutes, until almost cooked, but not soft. Drain well, rinse under cold water and drain thoroughly again.

2 Place the beaten eggs in a saucepan and cook over a gentle heat, stirring until softly scrambled.

3 Heat the oil in a preheated wok. Add the garlic, spring onions (scallions) and peas and sauté, stirring occasionally, for 1–2 minutes.

4 Stir the rice into the mixture in the pan, mixing to combine.

5 Add the eggs, soy sauce and salt to the wok and stir to mix the egg in well.

6 Transfer to serving dishes and garnish with the spring onion (scallion).

COOK'S TIP

The rice is rinsed under cold water to wash out the starch and prevent it from sticking together.

VARIATION

You may choose to add prawns (shrimp), ham or chicken in step 3, if you wish.

Cucumber & Beansprout Salad

Serves 4

INGREDIENTS

350 g/12 oz beansprouts
1 small cucumber
1 green (bell) pepper, seeded
  and cut into matchsticks
1 carrot, cut into matchsticks

2 tomatoes, finely chopped
1 celery stick, cut into
  matchsticks
1 garlic clove, crushed
dash of chilli sauce

2 tbsp light soy sauce
1 tsp wine vinegar
2 tsp sesame oil
16 fresh chives

1 Blanch the beansprouts in boiling water for 1 minute. Drain well and rinse under cold water. Drain thoroughly again.

2 Cut the cucumber in half lengthways. Scoop out the seeds with a teaspoon and discard. Cut the flesh into matchsticks and mix with the beansprouts, green (bell) pepper, carrot, tomatoes and celery.

3 Mix together the garlic, chilli sauce, soy sauce, vinegar and sesame oil. Pour the dressing over the vegetables, tossing well to coat. Spoon on to 4 individual serving plates. Garnish with fresh chives and serve.

COOK'S TIP

The vegetables may be prepared in advance, but do not assemble the dish until just before serving, otherwise the beansprouts will discolour.

VARIATION

You could substitute 350 g/12 oz cooked, cooled green beans or mangetout (snow peas) for the cucumber. Vary the beansprouts for a different flavour. Try aduki (adzuki) bean or alfalfa sprouts, as well as the better-known mung and soya beansprouts.

Special Fried Rice

Serves 4

INGREDIENTS

150 g/5^1/2 oz/^{2}/3 cup long-
    grain rice
2 tbsp vegetable oil
2 eggs, beaten
2 garlic cloves, crushed

1 tsp grated fresh root ginger
3 spring onions (scallions),
    sliced
75 g/3 oz/^{3}/4 cup cooked peas
150 g/5^1/2 oz/^{2}/3 cup
    beansprouts

225 g/8 oz/1^1/3 cups shredded
    ham
150 g/5^1/2 oz peeled, cooked
    prawns (shrimp)
2 tbsp light soy sauce

1 Cook the rice in a saucepan of boiling water for 15 minutes. Drain well, rinse under cold water and drain thoroughly again.

2 Heat 1 tablespoon of the oil in a preheated wok and add the beaten eggs and a further 1 teaspoon of oil. Tilt the wok so that the egg covers the base to make a thin pancake. Cook until lightly browned on the underside, then flip the pancake over and cook on the other side

for 1 minute. Remove from the wok and leave to cool.

3 Heat the remaining oil in the wok. Add the garlic and ginger and stir-fry for 30 seconds.

4 Add the spring onions (scallions), peas, beansprouts, ham and prawns (shrimp) and stir-fry for 2 minutes.

5 Stir in the soy sauce and rice and cook for a further 2 minutes. Transfer the rice to serving dishes.

6 Roll up the pancake, slice it very thinly and use to garnish the rice. Serve immediately.

COOK'S TIP

As this recipe contains meat and fish, it is ideal served with simpler vegetable dishes.

Chilli Pork Noodles

Serves 4

INGREDIENTS

350 g/12 oz minced
    (ground) pork
1 tbsp light soy sauce
1 tbsp dry sherry
350 g/12 oz egg noodles
2 tsp sesame oil
2 tbsp vegetable oil

2 garlic cloves, crushed
2 tsp grated fresh root ginger
2 fresh red chillies, sliced
1 red (bell) pepper, seeded and
    finely sliced
25 g/1 oz/$^1/_4$ cup unsalted
    peanuts

3 tbsp peanut butter
3 tbsp dark soy sauce
dash of chilli oil
300 ml/$^1/_2$ pint/1$^1/_4$ cups
    pork stock

1 Mix together the pork, light soy sauce and dry sherry in a large bowl. Cover and leave to marinate for 30 minutes.

2 Meanwhile, cook the noodles in a pan of boiling water for 4 minutes. Drain well, rinse in cold water and drain again.

3 Toss the noodles in the sesame oil.

4 Heat the vegetable oil in a preheated wok.

Add the garlic, ginger, chillies and red (bell) pepper and stir-fry for 30 seconds.

5 Add the pork to the mixture in the wok, together with the marinade. Continue cooking for about 1 minute, until the pork is sealed.

6 Add the peanuts, peanut butter, soy sauce, chilli oil and pork stock and cook for 2–3 minutes.

7 Toss the noodles in the mixture and serve at once.

VARIATION

Minced (ground) chicken or lamb would also be excellent in this recipe instead of the pork.

Beef Chow Mein

Serves 4

INGREDIENTS

450 g/1 lb egg noodles
4 tbsp peanut oil
450 g/1 lb lean beef steak, cut
  into thin strips
2 garlic cloves, crushed
1 tsp grated fresh root ginger

1 green (bell) pepper, thinly
  sliced
1 carrot, thinly sliced
2 celery sticks, sliced
8 spring onions (scallions)
1 tsp dark brown sugar

1 tbsp dry sherry
2 tbsp dark soy sauce
few drops of chilli sauce

1 Cook the noodles in a pan of boiling salted water for 4–5 minutes. Drain well, rinse under cold running water and drain thoroughly again.

2 Toss the noodles in 1 tablespoon of the oil.

3 Heat the remaining oil in a preheated wok. Add the beef and stir-fry for 3-4 minutes, stirring.

4 Add the garlic and ginger and stir-fry for 30 seconds.

5 Add the (bell) pepper, carrot, celery and spring onions (scallions) and stir-fry for 2 minutes.

6 Add the sugar, sherry, soy sauce and chilli sauce and cook, stirring, for 1 minute.

7 Stir in the noodles, mixing well, and cook until completely warmed through.

8 Transfer the noodles to warm serving bowls and serve immediately.

VARIATION

A variety of different vegetables may be used in this recipe for colour and flavour – try broccoli, red (bell) peppers, green beans or baby sweetcorn cobs.

Chicken on Crispy Noodles

Serves 4

INGREDIENTS

225 g/8 oz skinless, boneless
    chicken breasts, shredded
1 egg white
5 tsp cornflour (cornstarch)
225 g/8 oz thin egg noodles
320 ml/11 fl oz/1²/₃ cups
    vegetable oil

600 ml/1 pint/2¹/₂ cups
    chicken stock
2 tbsp dry sherry
2 tbsp oyster sauce
1 tbsp light soy sauce
1 tbsp hoisin sauce

1 red (bell) pepper, seeded and
    very thinly sliced
2 tbsp water
3 spring onions (scallions),
    chopped

1 Mix the chicken, egg white and 2 tsp of the cornflour (cornstarch) in a bowl. Let stand for at least 30 minutes.

2 Blanch the noodles in boiling water for 2 minutes, then drain. Heat 300 ml/¹/₂ pint of the oil in a preheated wok. Add the noodles, spreading them to cover the base of the wok. Cook over a low heat for about 5 minutes, until the noodles are browned on the underside. Flip the

noodles over and brown on the other side. Remove from the wok when crisp and browned, place on a serving plate and keep warm. Drain the oil from the wok.

3 Add 300 ml/¹/₂ pint/ 1¹/₄ cups of the stock to the wok. Remove from the heat and add the chicken, stirring well so that it does not stick. Return to the heat and cook for 2 minutes. Drain, discarding the stock.

4 Wipe the wok with kitchen paper (paper towels) and return to the heat. Add the sherry, oyster, soy, and hoisin sauces, (bell) pepper and the remaining stock and bring to the boil. Blend the remaining cornflour (cornstarch) with the water to form a paste and stir it into the mixture. Return the chicken to the wok and cook over a low heat for 2 minutes. Place the chicken on top of the noodles and sprinkle with spring onions (scallions).

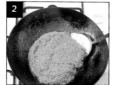
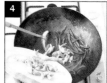

Banana Pastries

Serves 4

INGREDIENTS

DOUGH:
450 g/1 lb/4 cups plain (all-purpose) flour
60 g/2 oz/4 tbsp lard (shortening)
60 g/2 oz/4 tbsp unsalted butter

125 ml/4 fl oz/$^1/_2$ cup water
1 egg yolk, beaten
icing (confectioner's) sugar, for dusting
cream or ice cream, to serve

FILLING:
2 large bananas
75 g/2$^3/_4$ oz/$^1/_3$ cup finely chopped no-need-to-soak dried apricots
pinch of nutmeg
dash of orange juice

1 To make the dough, sift the flour into a large mixing bowl. Add the lard (shortening) and butter and rub into the flour with the fingertips until the mixture resembles breadcrumbs. Gradually blend in the water to make a soft dough. Wrap in cling film (plastic wrap) and chill in the refrigerator for 30 minutes.

2 Mash the bananas in a bowl with a fork and stir in the apricots, nutmeg and orange juice, mixing together well.

3 Roll the dough out on a lightly floured surface and cut out 16 × 10-cm/4-inch rounds.

4 Spoon a little of the banana filling on to one half of each round and fold the dough over the filling to make semi-circles. Pinch the edges together and seal them by pressing with the prongs of a fork.

5 Arrange the pastries on a non-stick baking tray (cookie sheet) and brush them with the beaten egg yolk.

6 Cut a small slit in each pastry and cook in a preheated oven, 180°C, 350°F/Gas 4, for about 25 minutes, or until golden brown.

7 Dust with icing (confectioner's) sugar and serve with cream or ice cream.

Poached Allspice Pears

Serves 4

INGREDIENTS

4 large, ripe pears
300 ml/$\frac{1}{2}$ pint/1$\frac{1}{4}$ cups
    orange juice

2 tsp ground allspice
60 g/2 oz/$\frac{1}{3}$ cup raisins
2 tbsp light brown sugar

grated orange rind, to
    decorate

1 Using an apple corer, core the pears. Using a sharp knife, peel the pears and cut them in half.

2 Place the pear halves in a large saucepan.

3 Add the orange juice, allspice, raisins and sugar to the pan and heat gently, stirring, until the sugar has dissolved. Bring the mixture to the boil for 1 minute.

4 Reduce the heat to low and leave to simmer for about 10 minutes, or until the pears are cooked,

but still fairly firm – test them by inserting the tip of a sharp knife.

5 Remove the pears from the pan with a slotted spoon and transfer to serving plates. Decorate and serve hot with the syrup.

VARIATION

Use cinnamon instead of the allspice and decorate with cinnamon sticks and fresh mint sprigs, if you prefer.

COOK'S TIP

The Chinese do not usually have desserts to finish off a meal, except at banquets and special occasions. Sweet dishes are usually served in between main meals as snacks, but fruit is refreshing at the end of a big meal.

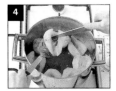

Chinese Custard Tarts

Makes 15

INGREDIENTS

DOUGH:
175 g/6 oz/1^1/2 cups plain
   (all-purpose) flour
3 tbsp caster (superfine) sugar
60 g/2 oz/4 tbsp unsalted
   butter

25 g/1 oz/2 tbsp lard
   (shortening)
2 tbsp water

CUSTARD:
2 small eggs

60 g/2 oz/^{1}/4 cup caster
   (superfine) sugar
175 ml/6 fl oz/^{3}/4 cup pint
   milk
^{1}/2 tsp ground nutmeg, plus
   extra for sprinkling
cream, to serve

1 To make the dough, sift the flour into a bowl. Add the sugar and rub in the butter and lard (shortening) until the mixture resembles breadcrumbs. Add the water and mix to form a dough.

2 Transfer the dough to a lightly floured surface and knead for 5 minutes, until smooth. Cover with cling film (plastic wrap) and leave to chill in the refrigerator while you prepare the filling.

3 To make the custard, beat the eggs and sugar together. Gradually add the milk and nutmeg and beat until well combined.

4 Separate the dough into 15 even-sized pieces. Flatten the dough pieces into rounds and press into shallow patty tins (pans).

5 Spoon the custard into the pastry cases (tart shells) and cook in a preheated oven, at 150°C/300°F/Gas Mark 2, for 25–30 minutes.

6 Transfer the tarts to a wire rack, leave to cool slightly, then sprinkle with nutmeg. Serve with cream.

COOK'S TIP

For extra convenience, make the dough in advance, cover and leave to chill in the refrigerator until required.

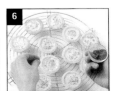

This is a Parragon Book
This edition published in 2002
Parragon
Queen Street House
4 Queen Street
Bath BA1 1HE, UK

ISBN: 0-75256-943-0

Printed in China

Note

Cup measurements in this book are for American cups. Tablespoons are assumed to be
15 ml. Unless otherwise stated, milk is assumed to be full fat, eggs are medium and
pepper is freshly ground black pepper.